THE INVENTOR
THROUGH HISTORY

Peter Lafferty and Julian Rowe
with illustrations
by Tony Smith and
Steve Wheele

Wayland

JOURNEY THROUGH HISTORY

The Builder Through History
The Explorer Through History
The Farmer Through History
The Inventor Through History
The Sailor Through History
The Soldier Through History

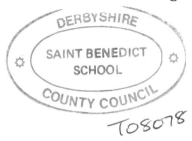
Series editor: William Wharfe
Editors: Rose Hill/Sue Hadden
Designer: Robert Wheeler

Typeset in the UK by Dorchester
Typesetting Group Ltd
Printed in Italy by G. Canale &
C.S.p.A., Turin
Bound in France by A.G.M.

First published in 1993 by
Wayland (Publishers) Limited
61 Western Road, Hove
East Sussex BN3 1JD, England

**British Library Cataloguing in
Publication Data**

Lafferty, Peter
    The Inventor Through History. –
(Journey Through History Series)
    I. Title   II. Rowe, Julian
    III. Smith, Tony IV. Series
    608.7

ISBN 0-7502-0436-2

Picture acknowledgements
The publisher wishes to thank the
following for supplying photographs
for use as illustrations in this book:
C M Dixon 6, 12; E.T. Archive 28;
Mary Evans Picture Library 12, 37,
38; Michael Holford 4, 14; Hulton
Picture Library cover, 24, 40;
Mansell Collection 26; Peter Newark
8, 9, 32; Ann Ronan Picture Library
10, 13, 14, 18, 20 (top), 22, 30, 34, 36;
The Science Museum 5; Tony Stone
Worldwide 17; Topham Picture
Library 29; Zefa cover, 16, 20
(below), 21, 33, 44, 45; other pictures
are in the Wayland Picture Library.
Artwork is by Tony Smith 7, 11, 15,
19, 23, 27, 31, 35, 39, 43 and Steve
Wheele 6, 16, 25, 29, 33, 37, 41.

Contents

Introduction

Who were the early inventors? Some we shall never know about. The wheel, which was invented about 5,000 years ago, changed the world – but there is no way of finding out who first made it. This book looks at some of the inventors we do know about, whose ideas have shaped our world.

There have been remarkably few inventors, considering how many millions of people have lived. Yet the vision and persistence of just these few have changed the way we all live. Inventors usually had (and still have) a hard time convincing other people that their ideas were of any use at all. They were often ridiculed, and only a very few became rich as a result of their inventions. The picture of the lone inventor, struggling against all the odds, is not far from the truth.

Three hundred years ago people led lives that were not very different from the lives of their parents or

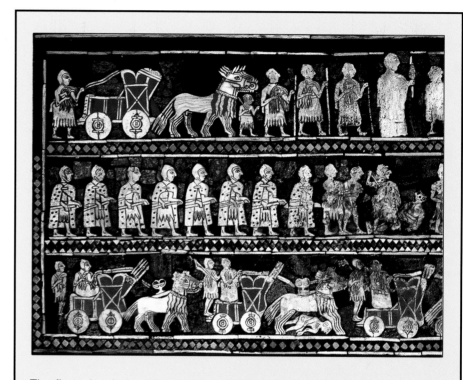

The first wheeled vehicle was probably some sort of cart. This picture from Mesopotamia shows a horse-drawn war cart. Its wheels are round-shaped sections of wooden plank, fixed together with wood or copper brackets. Lynch pins hold the wheels on to the axle. Later chariots had spoked wheels.

grandparents. The pace of life was slow and not much happened to change it. For more than a thousand years the horse and plough had dictated how people lived.

Agriculture was revolutionized at about 1730, when farmers began to use an improved plough that did more than scratch the surface of the soil. Food became easier to produce and was more plentiful. Perhaps there was a glimpse of the future when people began to use watermills and windmills to grind corn, and to work the bellows and hammers in smithies. For the first time there was something other than just muscle power to do the work.

Since the seventeenth century, every aspect of our lives has been changed by new inventions. At first the rate of change was slow, but in the twentieth century it has proceeded at bewildering speed, as modern technology has developed.

Look around you in any city today. The streets are full of cars and buses carrying people to work and school. The shops are stocked with goods that have come from all over the world. The fresh food you buy may have been growing thousands of kilometres away only a day or so ago. The newspapers report events that happened only hours before in a distant country. And life continues long after sunset in the brightly lit streets and buildings.

The inventions and discoveries that give us an easier way of life have been achieved over a comparatively short time. Some, however, have proved to be a mixed blessing. The energy we depend on from oil will not last for ever. The pollution caused by chemicals that we use can affect people's health, and destroy plant and animal life. Now and in the future we must be careful how we use the marvellous products of inventive genius described in the following pages.

THE NEW CENSUS OF THE UNITED STATES—THE ELECTRICAL ENUMERATING MECHANISM.—[See page 132.]

This illustration of the cover of the 30 August 1890 issue of *Scientific American* magazine shows an early forerunner of the computer. All the information from the 1890 US census was held on punched cards which the machine could quickly read. The machine halved the time taken, and saved half a million US dollars.

The computer, like the wheel, has transformed the world.

The first books

German goldsmith Johann Gutenberg, a person of many talents, made one of the greatest inventions of all times. In about 1438, he discovered a way of making metal type from which books could be printed. The type was made of pieces of metal with the raised shape of a reversed letter at one end. Pieces of type were arranged in groups to make words, and in lines to make sentences. The lines of type were clamped into position and wiped with

A page from the Bible printed by Johann Gutenberg in 1455, and coloured by hand.

Colourful books

The first book to be printed by Gutenberg was a textbook of Latin grammar produced in 1451. In 1455, he printed his first and only large book: a Bible. The first colour book was produced in Mainz in 1457 by Johann Fust and Peter Schöffer, who had been partners of Gutenberg. The colour was introduced by inking different sections of type with different coloured ink. In 1461 the first illustrated book was printed by Albrecht Pfister of Bamberg, Germany. The pictures were printed from engraved wooden blocks.

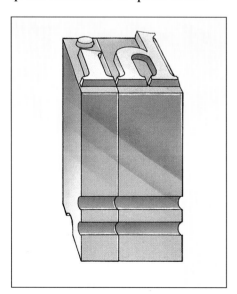

An example of type, metal blocks moulded into the mirror image of letters.

an inky rag. The ink clung to the raised surface of the type. When a piece of paper was pressed on to the inked type, the letters and words were printed on to the paper.

The idea behind Gutenberg's invention was not new. In the late 1300s, playing cards had been printed in Europe using carved wooden blocks, while the Chinese had used similar methods for hundreds of years. But Gutenberg was the first European to realize the importance of having movable type made up of individual letters. Furthermore, he had the metal-working skills to make the type. He developed an alloy – a mixture of tin and lead – that could be worked easily. He invented an ink which would cling to the type, and adapted a wine press to press the paper evenly on to the inked type. By about 1450, Gutenberg had perfected his techniques and began printing the first books.

Johann Gutenberg

Johann Gutenberg was born in about 1394 in Mainz, Germany. Not much is known about his early life, but it is thought he came from a well-off family; his father had an interest in a local mint. Perhaps because of this Gutenberg learnt the goldsmith's trade. In 1438, he began a printing business with a partner, Johann Fust. However, after a series of disagreements, the partnership was dissolved in 1455, with Fust taking possession of Gutenberg's printing equipment. Luckily, the most important book – the Bible – had already been printed. Gutenberg went on printing in Mainz, producing several smaller works until he retired in 1465. He died in 1468.

A fifteenth-century printing works. The master printer checks a proof of a page. Behind him is the press, adapted from a wine press.

Paper making

Paper was first made in the first century BC in China. The raw materials – fragments of bark, cloth or fishnets – were beaten to a pulp and mixed with water. The mixture was spread on screens, dried and hardened. The secret of paper making found its way to Europe by an accident of war. In AD 751, the Chinese attacked the Arab city of Samarkand in central Asia. In the attack, a Chinese papermaker was taken prisoner and forced to reveal the process.

Around 1300 BC, the Chinese used 'chops', or seals engraved with the king's signature, for stamping official documents. This led to the printing of books from blocks of wood carved with a raised passage of text. When the wood was coated with ink, paper was pressed on by hand. This process is called letterpress printing. In AD 770, the Japanese Empress Shotoku ordered a million prayer sheets to be printed in this way. It took printers six years to complete the task.

Movable type – small blocks with a single character carved on the end – was invented in China by Pi Sheng during the 1040s. Pi used blocks baked from clay, held in place in an iron frame by paste. Later, in 1403, longer-lasting metal type was developed. However, the Chinese system of writing has a character for each word, so thousands of different printing characters were required. European writing systems, which use an alphabet with a small number of letters, were much easier to set in type. This explains why printing spread so quickly through Europe once Gutenberg had hit upon the idea of movable type. The book publishing industry was born.

Before the introduction of printing, books were copied by hand. This was a slow and costly process. When printing was introduced to Europe by Gutenberg, new works could be published much more cheaply. The Bible and classical literature quickly found their way into print. Books of stories, such as Chaucer's *Canterbury Tales* and Malory's *Le Morte Darthur* (printed in 1485) appeared, along with works of history and medicine.

An early fifteenth-century handwritten version of Chaucer's Canterbury Tales. Printing made books like this more widely available.

Der Papyrer.

Ich brauch Hadern zu meiner Mül
Dran treibt mirs Rad deß wassers viel/
Daß mir die zschnitn Hadern nelt/
Das zeug wirt in wasser einquelt/
Drauß mach ich Pogn/auff dē filtz bring/
Durch preß das wasser darauß zwing.
Denn henck ichs auff/laß drucken wern/
Schneweiß vnd glatt/so hat mans gern.

Der Buchbinder.

Ich bind allerley Bücher ein/
Geistlich vnd Weltlich/groß vnd klein/
In Perment oder Bretter nur
Vnd beschlags mit guter Clausur
Vnd Spangen/vnd stempff sie zur zier/
Ich sie auch im anfang planier/
Etlich vergüld ich auff dem schnitt/
Da verdien ich viel geldes mit.

Der Buchdrücker.

Ich bin geschicket mit der preß
So ich aufftrag den Firniß reß/
So bald mein dienr den bengel zuckt/
So ist ein bogn papyrs gedruckt.
Da durch kombt manche Kunst an tag/
Die man leichtlich bekommen mag.
Vor zeiten hat man die bücher gschribn/
Zu Meintz die Kunst ward erstlich triebn.

Producing a book in the sixteenth century. This old German print shows the workshops of a papermaker (left), book binder (middle), and printer (right).

William Caxton

William Caxton, born in 1422, became the first English printer. He started a printing works in London in 1476. His first book was about the sayings of wise men. He also printed many books of poetry and stories, such as the story of King Arthur. In fifteen years, he printed ninety-four different books. As a linguist he translated twenty of the books that he printed from foreign languages. His work did much to standardize the English language. He died in 1491.

The early books were in Latin, the language used by scholars. But soon printers realized a need for books in the languages of the common people. However, language varied considerably within a country. Printers were forced to choose one version or dialect of a language for their books, and this helped lead to the standardization of languages. For instance, William Caxton, England's first printer, used the dialect spoken in the south-east of England, and this in time developed into modern English.

Once books were more widely available, the ideas of new thinkers could spread quickly. The ideas of early Greek thinkers were rediscovered during the fifteenth and sixteenth centuries, leading to a period of great intellectual activity called the Renaissance. In 1543, Nicolaus Copernicus' book proving that the Earth moved around the Sun was published, challenging the accepted view of the universe. Isaac Newton's book on the universe *Principia* was printed in 1687, starting an age of scientific discovery.

9

The steam age

In 1763, James Watt sat in his workshop at the University of Glasgow, repairing a small model of a steam engine. The engine had been invented in 1705 by a Devon blacksmith, Thomas Newcomen. Newcomen's engine was used to pump water out of coal and tin mines. It looked like a pump, with a piston moving up and down inside a cylinder.

Watt quickly saw that the engine was crude and inefficient. Instead of producing useful power, most of the heat supplied to the engine was wasted. Watt reasoned that the engine would produce much more power if the steam could be condensed in a separate chamber connected to the cylinder. Otherwise the cylinder had to be reheated after each piston stroke. He immediately undertook a series of experiments to test his ideas.

It took Watt over a year to find a way to improve Newcomen's design. Eventually Watt manufactured his improved engine. He formed a business partnership in 1774 with Matthew Boulton who encouraged Watt in his development of the engine. It was installed in factories and mines across Britain. The engine was one of the driving forces of the Industrial Revolution – the explosion of industrial and manufacturing activity that occurred in Britain between 1750 and 1850.

Watt's steam engine

Watt's steam engine was similar to Newcomen's engine but it had two cylinders. One cylinder was always hot and one always cold. The piston moved up and down inside the hot, or power, cylinder. When the piston was at the top of the cylinder, a valve opened allowing the steam to flow into the second cylinder, or condenser, where it condensed, (turned back into water). Because the power cylinder was not allowed to cool, valuable fuel was not wasted in reheating it before each movement of the piston.

Newcomen's engine

In Newcomen's engine, the piston rose as steam flowed into the cylinder. When the piston was at the top of the cylinder, water was sprayed into the cylinder, condensing the steam. This created a vacuum under the piston and air pressure forced the piston down. More steam then flowed into the cylinder and the process was repeated. The problem with Newcomen's engine was that the cylinder was cooled each time water was sprayed in. Then the cylinder had to be heated up again before steam could flow in. This used extra fuel.

Newcomen's steam engine of 1705. The boiler is at (a), the piston (h) is in the cylinder (c). This engine used the power of atmospheric pressure rather than steam pressure. It needed a lot of coal.

James Watt

James Watt was born in Greenock in the west of Scotland in 1736. He trained first to be a mechanic and then as a mathematical instrument maker at the University of Glasgow. He gave up his work at the University to concentrate on building steam engines. Over the years, Watt gradually improved his engine, inventing a 'governor' to control the speed, and a system of gears, called a sun and planet gear. These converted the up and down motion of the engine into a more useful turning motion. When he died in 1819, the steam age was already well-established.

James Watt in his workshop, watching a model beam engine work. He realized that the engine wasted most of its heat energy as the cylinder was cooled.

The steam age

In 1750, most people in Britain lived in the countryside, raising sheep and cattle or growing crops. Others practised rural crafts, as blacksmiths, thatchers or wheelwrights. Roads were poor and most people did not travel far from their home village.

This picture was changed forever by the invention of the first reliable source of power – the steam engine. Previously, water wheels and windmills were used to turn grindstones, pump water, work furnace bellows and operate saw mills. Where there was no wind or water power, muscle power – either human or animal – had to be used. These sources of power had grave disadvantages: muscle power was puny, and wind and water were unreliable. Water-driven mills had to stop work if the water stopped flowing.

The steam engine meant that factory owners could operate large machines on a regular basis. So large factories were built in towns, using steam-driven spinning and weaving machines, or giant metal-working machines. Mines could be sunk deeper because the steam engine could pump out water from the deepest mine. Workers moved into towns to be near the factories and so the towns grew larger. All these changes combined to create the Industrial Revolution, which James Watt's steam engine helped to begin.

An 1895 steam engine used to pump water from a tin mine at Cambourne, Cornwall, England. The engine is inside the building.

An 1840 drawing showing the working conditions in a cloth mill at the time. The children are kept hard at work by supervisors with canes.

During the Industrial Revolution, children as young as four years old were sent to work in factories and mines. In a government report of 1842, little Fanny Drake described her work in a mine: 'I had to hurry, up to the calves of my legs in water. It was as bad as this for a fortnight at a time . . . My feet were skinned, and just as if they were scalded, for the water was bad . . . I was off my work owing to it, and had a headache and bleeding at my nose.'

In about 1800, Richard Trevithick, a Cornish engineer, invented a new kind of steam engine which produced far more power from a smaller engine. It used high-pressure steam and was small and powerful enough to be mounted on wheels. In 1802 Trevithick used the new powerful engine to haul loaded wagons along rails. Through the steam engine the railway age had begun.

The railway engine, or locomotive, was developed by British engineer George Stephenson. In 1825, he made a locomotive using the high-pressure engine to carry passengers. It was called *Locomotion* and carried passengers between Stockton and Darlington, in north-east England. In

1829, Stephenson developed a locomotive called *The Rocket*, which reached a speed of 46 km per hour. This was faster than a horse could run. Some people thought that it might be impossible for travellers to breathe at these high speeds.

After this success, Stephenson was asked to build other railways. The railways spread fast between the years 1830 and 1840. Lines were soon built from London to all the main towns. In 1835 there were only 800 km of track; by 1845 there were nearly 6,500 km and by 1850 there were 16,000 km. George Stephenson's son, Robert, helped in the work, building railways in England and abroad and many fine bridges.

Richard Trevithick's *Catch-me-who-can*

In 1808, Richard Trevithick built a locomotive to carry passengers, called *Catch-me-who-can*. The locomotive ran on a small circular track in London, near the site of the present-day Euston railway station. People paid a small amount for a ride. The train was great fun, and could travel at a speed of 20 km per hour. However, it made little money for Trevithick.

Travelling on the Liverpool and Manchester railway 1831. First-class carriages are shown at the top drawn by the locomotive *Jupiter*. The last carriage (not shown) carried the mail. Below are second and third-class carriages drawn by *North Star*. The first and second class carriages were constructed after the style of three stagecoach bodies combined to form one carriage. The guard rode on top of the first carriage and directed the engine driver.

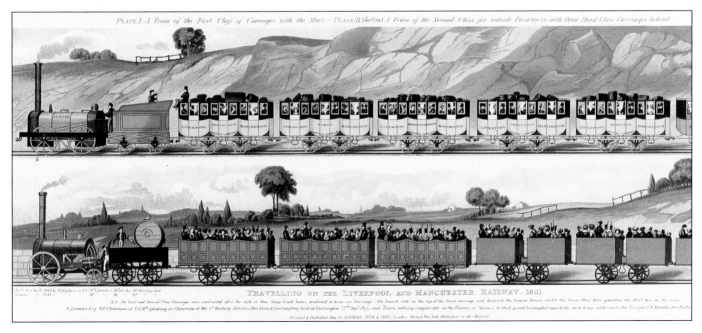

The age of electricity

When Michael Faraday invented a machine that could make electricity in 1831, the prime minister of Britain, Sir Robert Peel, asked him what use it would be. Faraday is said to have replied, 'I don't know, but I'll wager that one day your government will tax it.'

Early in the nineteenth century, electricity was still a mystery. Then, in 1820, a Danish scientist, Hans Oersted, discovered the first important clue. He placed a magnetic compass beside a wire carrying an electric current and saw that its needle turned, so that it was no longer pointing North. This effect, he and other scientists recognized, linked electricity to magnetism.

The young Michael Faraday became convinced that magnetism could also produce electricity. In 1831, after many experiments with two coils of wire wrapped around the same iron ring, he showed that the magnetism produced by electricity

flowing in one coil of wire could set up an electric current in the other. By demonstrating that a moving magnet could do the same thing, Faraday invented the dynamo, a device that changed the world.

Hans Oersted discovered that an electric current near a hanging magnet caused the magnet to move.

A selection of Michael Faraday's original coils, in different shapes. The wires on the coils carried an electric current set up when a magnet was moved towards a coil.

Electric power

In 1831 Michael Faraday showed that motion and magnetism produced electricity. A year later the Frenchman Hyppolyte Pixii made the first practical dynamo and the modern electrical industry was born. The first power station, driven by water, generated electricity to light the streets of Godalming, in south-east England, in 1881. Twelve years later the power of Niagara Falls was harnessed to generate electricity. Such hydroelectric power schemes are now found throughout the world.

Michael Faraday lecturing at the Royal Institution, in London. He was particularly interested in the education of children, and started a series of Christmas lectures for children. These lectures are still given and appear on television.

Michael Faraday

Michael Faraday was born in 1791, the son of a poor blacksmith. He had almost no education – just enough to learn to read and write and do a little arithmetic. At the age of thirteen he began to work for a local bookseller. He liked best the books that described experiments in chemistry and electricity. As he read, Faraday made notes, and soon he was certain that what he wanted more than anything was to become a scientist. He applied to work at the Royal Institution in London, and the research he did there led to the invention of the electric motor, the transformer and the dynamo. Faraday was one of the world's greatest scientists, but he was always a modest man. He accepted, with reluctance, the honours and awards that were showered on him, and when he died in 1867 his grave was marked with the simplest of headstones.

The age of electricity

When Michael Faraday was a young man, the city streets were dimly lit by gas lamps. Gas lamps also provided light in homes and in theatres, but often caused fires. One hundred years later, through Faraday's dynamo working in power stations, streets and homes were safely and brightly lit by electric lighting.

The twentieth century has been the age of electricity. No other single development has had such an enormous effect on our lives. At a flick of a switch we can light our homes, cook food or entertain ourselves. Most of the goods we buy are produced in factories that use electricity. In illness we depend on electricity to power medical equipment in hospitals, and our health depends on refrigerators that preserve our food.

The first light bulb

Joseph Swan in England and Thomas Edison in America invented the first reliable electric light bulb in 1878. The two men disputed who patented this invention first, but later joined forces to form the Edison and Swan Electric Light Company. The electric light bulb that screws into its socket was invented by Edison.

Refining filaments

Two Americans were responsible for improving the filaments in electric light bulbs. In 1882 Lewis Latimer, the son of a runaway slave, found a better way to make electric bulb filaments and also wrote the first book on electric lighting. He later became the chief engineer in charge of installing electric light plants in New York and Philadelphia. William Coolidge invented the tungsten filament in 1908, and this is still used in light bulbs today.

New York city lit up at night by electricity.

A range of electrical goods for sale in a department store. How many different kinds can you see?

Electricity is needed for transport – for cars, trains and signalling systems, the navigation of ships and planes, lifts and escalators. Communications systems are powered by electricity – television, radio, satellites, computers, telephones and fax machines. The exploration of space and all kinds of scientific research require electricity. Every year, more and more uses for electricity are being discovered. The age of electricity has really only just begun.

Generating all the electricity we need uses an enormous amount of energy. Since the Industrial Revolution much energy has been produced by burning coal, and big power stations still burn coal to turn water into steam. The steam powers the turbines that drive the electric generators.

Burning coal produces the gas carbon dioxide. The amount of carbon dioxide in the air has increased by 15 per cent in the last hundred years. This is thought to have an important effect on the Earth's temperature.

Carbon dioxide allows heat energy from the Sun to pass through it to the Earth, but traps the heat radiated back from the Earth's surface so it does not escape into space. This is known as the greenhouse effect. Scientists think that the increasing amounts of carbon dioxide in the air through human activity may cause the Earth's temperature to rise rapidly within the next century. Because we now understand the harm that carbon dioxide can cause, governments are looking for ways to reduce the amount that each country produces.

Today's scientists and inventors are looking for safe and clean ways to generate electricity. One way is to use 'renewable' sources of energy, such as water, solar or wind power. Many people think that nuclear energy would be the answer, if we could be sure there was no danger of nuclear accidents. New power stations are much more efficient, and make better use of natural gas and oil. But this is only a short-term answer, because like coal, gas and oil are fossil fuels. They will run out at some time in the future.

Long-distance communications

'Come here, Mr Watson, I want to see you.' These were the first words heard on a telephone. They were spoken by Alexander Graham Bell to his assistant, Thomas Watson, in 1876. Both men were working long hours, trying to make their electrical telephone work. Watson, who was in the next room, replied, 'I can hear you . . . perfect . . . wonderful!'

When the world's first telephone conversation took place, long-distance communication by telegraph was already being widely used. The first practical system had been developed by the American Joseph Henry in 1831, and an undersea telegraph cable was laid between Britain and the USA in 1866. But the telegraph could only be used for coded messages. At that time all attempts to transmit the human voice along a wire had been unsuccessful.

The problem was how to transform the vibrations of the human voice into electric signals. Bell and Watson achieved this with a thin membrane that had a piece of metal attached to the centre. When sound waves hit the membrane, it vibrated the metal. This set off an electric current in a magnetic coil. At the receiving end the same apparatus converted the electric signals back into sound.

Thanks to Bell's invention, it is now possible to talk to anyone in the world, merely by dialling numbers.

The main telegraph station in London 1882, showing the operator receiving a message on the ticker-tape machine.

The telegraph

The first telegraphic code, invented by Samuel Morse in 1837, used dots and dashes to represent the letters of the alphabet. Morse, who was an American portrait painter, patented his electric telegraph unaware that Charles Wheatstone and William Cook in England had also invented a practical electric telegraph. Later, in 1855, a printing telegraph was used. This led to the telex machine, which after 1936 enabled subscribers to send and receive typed messages directly.

18

Alexander Graham Bell

Alexander Graham Bell was born in Edinburgh, Scotland, in 1847. Both his father and his grandfather were authorities on elocution, or correct speaking. When the family moved to the USA, Alexander began to devote himself to teaching the deaf and dumb. He also became interested in increasing the efficiency of the telegraph system, using his knowledge of sound. It was this work that led to the invention of the telephone. The scientific unit for measuring the intensity of sound, the bell, is named after him. He died in 1922.

Alexander Graham Bell speaks to his assistant, Thomas Watson, on the first telephone. The early telephones were difficult to use. Speakers had to shout to be heard even over short distances. Many people did not see the point of having telephones since, in those days, servants could be used to carry messages.

Before the invention of the telegraph and telephone, news generally travelled at the speed of a horse. True, there were exceptions. The ancient Greeks used mirrors to flash signals from hilltop to hilltop. In times of danger, beacons were lit to warn of the approaching enemy. But such methods were of limited use.

Today, the world of business depends on rapid communication of information. Families and friends can stay in touch with one another by talking on the telephone. The fire or the ambulance service can be called instantly in an emergency.

Two years after the first telephone conversation, the first telephone exchange opened in New Haven, Connecticut, USA. Today, satellites at a height of 35,700 km in space link the continents of the world. They have largely replaced the submarine telephone cables the first of which had been laid in 1956 across the Atlantic.

Many new uses have been found for the telephone system. The facsimile machine (fax) can transmit pages of text or illustration by telephone faster than any postal

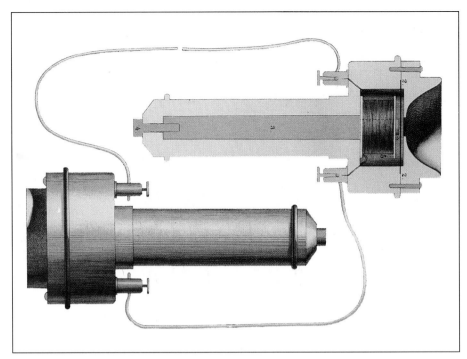

Above An early Bell telephone. The same apparatus was used for both speaking and listening. This meant a lot of swapping round during a conversation. Later a separate transmitter (into which one spoke) and a receiver (through which the message came) were designed.

Optical fibres. The first fibre optic telephone line was opened in 1977 in Hertfordshire, England. Messages carried by optical fibre travel at the speed of light, 300,000 kilometres per second.

Fibre optics

During the late 1970s the traditional copper wires that carry telephone messages were being replaced by optical fibres – very fine strands of glass bound up in a protective coating. Fibre optic cables transmit pulses of light generated by a laser. This application of fibre optics can transmit thousands of telephone conversations at the same time and can also carry television signals.

service. It does this by turning light reflected from a page of writing into electrical signals that can be transmitted along telephone lines.

Computers, connected to telephone lines by devices called modems, exchange information between cities, countries or continents. In this way a person can access information held on a database of a computer on the other side of the world. Miniature portable radiotelephones have revolutionized business communication – no longer is the busy executive tied to the office, or unable to communicate while stuck in a traffic jam.

Telephone lines are used daily to transmit television pictures together with sound, so that conferences between people in different countries can take place at the same time. Already, researchers are working on computerized telephone systems that can translate from one language to another. As a result for example a Japanese person in Tokyo will be able to talk to an American colleague in Chicago without either knowing the other's language.

Alexander Bell, who was

A microwave tower. Many telephone calls are transmitted over land and to satellites using microwaves.

a tireless promoter of his invention, could hardly have imagined the many different uses that have since been devised for the telephone.

The talking machine

Many inventors are famous because of a single invention. Thomas Alva Edison patented nearly 1,300 inventions. He declared, 'Genius is one per cent inspiration and 99 per cent perspiration'. He created an 'inventions factory' in Menlo Park, New Jersey, USA and filled 3,500 notebooks with ideas, often working twenty hours a day. When asked about his retirement he replied, 'I'll retire the day before my funeral.'

Edison's own favourite invention was the phonograph, or sound recorder. He is chiefly remembered for this invention, and for developing electric lighting. In the late 1870s the first phonograph, or gramophone, did not look much like today's hi-tech gadgets. It consisted of a cylinder of tinfoil, and a sharp needle, or stylus, that cut a groove in the metal foil as it rotated. The movements of the stylus were controlled by a simple microphone which picked up the changes in air pressure caused by sound. To hear the recording, the stylus was moved to the beginning of the groove, and the cylinder moved by being cranked round by hand.

The world's first talking machine sold for $18, and Edison thought it would be used in offices to take dictation. He never imagined all its uses.

A woman is recording cylinders to put into talking dolls in about 1890.

The first words recorded by Edison on his phonograph in 1877 were 'Halloo, halloo'. The following year he formed a company to market the machine. However, the sound from the metal cylinder was very poor. Chichester Bell, a cousin of the inventor of the telephone, developed a wax cylinder that greatly improved the quality. The flat disc was demonstrated by German inventor Emile Berliner in 1888. His phonograph was intended from the start to play pre-recorded discs. And so the modern recording industry had started.

Thomas Alva Edison

Thomas Alva Edison was born in 1847 in Milan, Ohio, USA. He had hardly any schooling but from an early age was full of curiosity and bright ideas. His first job, at the age of twelve, was selling newspapers on a train. He also produced his own journal on a second-hand printing press in the luggage van. This first venture was followed by hundreds of others throughout his long life. His inventions included an early form of moving pictures, a machine that counted election votes, and a method of propelling helicopters using explosives. In 1879 he produced the first electric filament light bulb, and soon many houses were lit with Edison bulbs . When he died in 1931 lights throughout the USA were dimmed in his honour.

Thomas Alva Edison with an early phonograph. The sound produced was so weak that special earphones had to be used. He kept a bed in his laboratory in Menlo Park, New York, so that he could spend all his time inventing. He became known as the 'wizard of Menlo Park'.

The talking machine

Recorded music is now part of our daily lives. Radio stations play it all day. It is played in lifts, airports, restaurants and doctors' waiting rooms. Many people have collections of records, tapes and, increasingly, compact discs (CDs).

Until 1925 all the performers had to crowd round a large horn to make a recording. Each record played for only a few minutes and the sound quality was poor and scratchy. Then Joseph Maxfield at Bell Telephone Laboratories in New Jersey, USA, invented an electrical system using an electronic microphone to capture the sound. This made high-quality recording possible.

Before the invention of the phonograph, people made their own music. Few ever heard famous artists performing. Now millions of people know exactly what the latest group sounds like. Two improvements made this possible: the long-playing record made of plastic, which was first produced in 1948 by Columbia, an American company, and stereophonic recordings. Stereo records appeared in 1958, based on earlier experiments by Alan Dower Blumlein at EMI in Britain. Here at last was a method of recording that could produce sound exactly like the original performance.

The first records were made from a wax master disc. Now, the original

Edison's improved phonograph recording during a festival at the Crystal Palace, 1888.

recording is made on magnetic tape. Mistakes can be corrected by re-recording. Special effects are often used to enhance the recordings, particularly on pop records. The final recording may be very different from a live performance, with brighter sounds and a different balance between the backing instruments.

The Dutch electronics group Philips gave an enormous boost to the recording industry in the 1960s with the invention of the tape cassette. Following the invention of the transistor, tape recorders became more reliable, inexpensive and smaller. In the 1980s, the tiny 'Walkman' was developed, which lets people listen to recorded music wherever they are – eating, jogging, sun-bathing and even swimming.

Now both tapes and long-playing records are being successfully challenged by the compact disc, which first appeared in 1982. This newest chapter in the story of the talking machine produces sound of astonishing clarity. Because the impressions on the disc are read by light from a miniature laser, playing the disc does not wear it out. The sound is recorded using a computer. CD players depend on computer techniques to

A modern compact disc (CD) player and a gramophone of the 1890s. The gramophone was wound up using the handle at the side. It had no amplification apart from the listening horn.

translate the computer signals back into sound. Sound recording has come a long way from Edison's original hand-cranked phonograph.

Compact discs

The long-playing record was originally promoted as being unbreakable, unlike the earlier records. But unfortunately it is easy to scratch, and then it becomes unplayable. Tape cassettes are small and easy to carry, but the tape can tangle and break. Compact discs are durable and scratches on the surface do not affect the quality of sound reproduction.

On the road

One day early in 1885 Karl Benz wheeled a strange contraption on to the cinder path outside his workshop in Mannheim, Germany. The vehicle looked rather like a large three-wheeled pram, with a petrol engine behind the seat. Leaping aboard, Benz made four circuits of the path, cheered on by his wife and a small crowd of employees, before a chain snapped and the vehicle came to a standstill. Benz had become the first person to build and run a petrol-driven car.

In Mannheim at that time 'conveyances driven by prime energy' were banned from being driven on the roads. Benz asked the authorities for permission to take his car out on to the streets, and when they finally agreed he caused a sensation by driving at 14.4 km an hour. At another public display he managed to achieve the first car accident – in his excitement he forgot to steer and collided with a brick wall.

In 1865, a law in Britain required every motor car to be preceded by a person carrying a red flag. Motorists mocked the law by having boys carrying tiny flags – as in this print of a Benz car in 1894.

Benz sold his first car in 1887. By the next year he was employing fifty men in his workshop to make cars for sale. A four-wheeled vehicle was manufactured in 1893, and soon Benz was selling 500 a year.

Karl Benz

Karl Benz was born in Karlsruhe, Germany, in 1844. His father, one of the first locomotive drivers in Germany, died when Karl was two years old. Benz studied engineering at the Karlsruhe Polytechnic and then set up a company in Mannheim to manufacture engines powered by gas. He built his first motor vehicle in 1885. When he became aware that another German inventor, Gottlieb Daimler, was also making motor vehicles, a bitter rivalry developed between the two men. However, three years before Benz died in 1926, their two companies merged to manufacture Mercedes-Benz cars.

The Benz 'Patent Motor Wagon'. At the time, German newspaper *Mannheimer Zeitung* described his invention as 'useless, ridiculous and indecent'. It asked, 'Who is interested in such a contrivance as a horseless carriage, so long as there are horses for sale?'

German pioneers developed the first motor cars. Two Frenchmen, René Panhard and Emile Levassor, worked on the design and produced the first 'modern' motor car in 1891. It had an engine at the front under a bonnet, a gear-box, a foot-controlled clutch and a rear wheel drive – all of which are still used in cars today. The bonnet allowed room for a larger engine that gave more power. By the turn of the century, extravagant, luxurious limousines, such as the Rolls-Royce 'Silver Ghost', were being custom-built for those who could afford them.

In the USA Henry Ford started to make cars that ordinary people could afford. The Model T Ford, nicknamed 'Tin Lizzie', was the first car to be mass-produced. By 1927 fifteen million of them had come off the production line, helping the USA to become the most powerful economic and industrial country in the world. In the 1930s Britain became the second largest car-manufacturing nation. The Austin Seven and the 'Bullnose' Morris Cowley

Other inventors

While Benz was working on his first motor vehicle, other inventors were experimenting along similar lines. An Austrian, Siegfried Marcus, invented the first engine that used petrol as a fuel. It was a two-stroke engine, one in which every second stroke of the engine produces power. Two Germans, Nikolaus Otto and Eugen Langen, built a more powerful four-stroke engine in 1876. This was further developed by one of their employees, Gottlieb Daimler. The four-stroke engine is the most generally used system in cars today.

brought car ownership within reach of the ordinary family. Also in the 1930s, the German Volkswagen ('people's car') was put into production.

Since the Second World War the demand for motor cars has soared dramatically. The car is now the most popular means of transport for millions of people. In the developed countries of the world, almost every family owns at least one vehicle, and often two. The motor car has revolutionized our way of life by giving us the freedom to live, work, shop and travel to wherever we wish to go.

However, along with rapid change, the motor car has also brought with it many problems. Many more roads have been constructed, and areas of

The production line for the Model T at Ford Motors in 1910.

lovely countryside are now criss-crossed with a network of motorways. Car accidents are a frequent cause of death, and pollution from exhaust fumes affects the environment and people's health. As more and more people become car-owners, traffic jams are getting longer and the roar of city traffic more deafening to our ears.

However, the automobile industry is very important to the economy of many countries. Japan now manufactures more cars than any other single country, including the USA. As well as producing goods to sell at home and abroad, the industry also supports a wide range of other businesses, such as petrol stations, hotels and shopping and leisure centres, built away from the centre of cities.

A 1934 advertisement shows the motor car as part of the lifestyle of the rich.

Battery

The electric car

The world's natural resources are limited, and since the 1970s manufacturers have been designing cars that use less oil. Benz's petrol-driven motor car may eventually be replaced by vehicles that run on different fuels. For some years inventors have been working on designs for electric cars. An efficient battery that is light as well as long-lasting has yet to be properly developed.

Signals without wires

The imagination of the world was caught when the first radio signal crossed the Atlantic in 1901. This feat was due to the genius of the Italian inventor, Guglielmo Marconi. His transmitter at Poldhu in Cornwall, England, sent the signal – three dots for the letter S in Morse code – which was received in Canada, at St John's, Newfoundland. Marconi had proved long-distance radio communication was possible.

A German physicist, Heinrich Hertz, demonstrated the existence of radio waves in 1888. When Marconi read about this, he was determined to try and invent a system for transmitting messages by them. He succeeded in making a bell ring by sending a radio signal across the attic of his parents' home. More ambitious experiments followed and by 1895, Marconi had invented a practical system of wireless telegraphy.

From the towers at Poldhu, Cornwall, Marconi sent the first radio signal from England to America.

The Italian government ridiculed his invention, so Marconi moved to England and continued to improve his system until he succeeded in sending a message across the Channel to France.

The British Government decided to take up Marconi's invention as an aid to shipping. The first radio signals were in Morse code only. These could not be tuned, but Marconi soon found a way to tune the receiver to a particular transmitter. Already by 1915, speech had been transmitted across the Atlantic, using the new radio valves developed in the USA.

Marconi was awarded the Nobel Prize for his work in 1909. King George V of England knighted him and the Italians, who had initially rejected his ideas, showered him with honours.

Guglielmo Marconi with his transmitting apparatus. In 1898 he became famous when he radioed medical bulletins to Queen Victoria when the Prince of Wales was ill.

Guglielmo Marconi

Guglielmo Marconi was born in Bologna, Italy, in 1874. His father was a banker and his mother an heiress to the Jameson Irish whiskey fortune. Marconi's mother encouraged him in his experiments with electricity and magnets and always spoke English to him, which was a great advantage when he set off to England to interest the British Government in his invention. Unlike many inventors, Marconi became rich and famous. He died in 1937.

The liner *Titanic* sank on its maiden voyage in 1912, after striking an iceberg. The 703 survivors were rescued by another liner, the *Carpathia*, which had picked up the new SOS signal by radio.

When radio was still a novelty, Marconi predicted, 'Perhaps some day everyone will have a receiver in their house and, from a central station, news of all kinds will be constantly sent out . . .'. That was in 1914. How the air became filled with radio waves is the story of modern worldwide communication.

Radio, television and telephone are used by nearly everyone today. Industrial societies depend on good and instant communication, and radio signals travel at the speed of light. Ordinarily, the listener is not aware of any delay because radio waves travel at 300,000 km per second. However, when US astronauts spoke from the Moon to Earth 385,000 km away, there was a noticeable delay of just over a second.

Now three satellites, like artificial moons above the Pacific, Atlantic and Indian Oceans, relay radio signals to and from most places on Earth. These satellites carry international telephone calls. People can keep in touch easily because most calls can now be dialled directly from one country to another. Computers and facsimile (fax) machines increasingly use the same telephone links.

The exploration of space depends on sending and receiving radio signals over vast distances. The radio signals from a spacecraft travelling to the edge of the solar system are very weak

Dr Crippen, the London wife-killer, was aboard the liner *Montrose* in 1910. He was escaping to Quebec with his girlfriend, Ethel Le Neve. The captain became suspicious and sent a Marconigram to the police in London. Dr Crippen was arrested on arrival in Canada. He was the first murderer to be caught by radio.

and difficult to interpret. Space scientists have computers to help them build up accurate pictures of distant planets.

In the early days of radio, the signal was often weak and distorted by electrical interference on Earth. This problem was overcome in 1917 by two inventions by Major Edwin Armstrong of the US Army. The first was a radio receiver called a superheterodyne. Such a radio is more sensitive to weak signals and can be selectively tuned. The second was a new method of transmitting radio signals, called frequency

Early radio

In 1920 the Marconi company gave the first public radio broadcasts. Although the programmes were very dull, listeners were excited and soon there was a huge demand for wireless sets. In 1922 the British Broadcasting Corporation (BBC) was formed and began to broadcast regular programmes. Its first studio was a small room above a shop in London. Within a few years broadcasting stations were established in many other countries, and soon a radio network linked the world. A new form of entertainment could be enjoyed by everyone in their own home.

modulation. This largely eliminated interference, or static, caused by electrical storms.

Steady development of radio since then has led to stereophonic radio broadcasting. Small, portable radios became a possibility when the transistor was invented. The transistor is also used in car telephone systems, paging devices, homing devices to follow migrating birds and animals, and in radio-controlled model cars and aeroplanes.

When Marconi died, many countries ceased broadcasting for two minutes in tribute to him.

Above Astronaut James Irwin on the Moon during the Apollo 15 mission in 1971. The radio aerial can be seen on the Lunar Rover at the right.

A modern satellite can carry several hundred thousand calls and several television programmes at the same time.

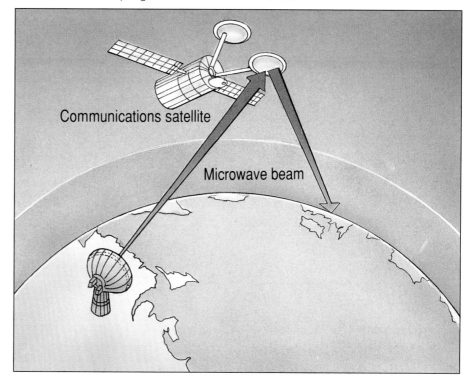

Communications satellite

Microwave beam

Into the air

On 17 December 1903, at Kitty Hawk in North Carolina, Orville Wright lay precariously across the wing of a primitive aircraft, clasping the controls. His brother Wilbur ran alongside, gripping one wing to keep it steady. The biplane, called *Flyer*, bumped slowly forward and rose 3 metres into the air. It travelled about 36 metres before diving into the sands. This was the first mechanical flight. It had lasted 12 seconds. Despite its time, the flight was historic because until then only gliders had travelled through the air.

For the Wright brothers, it was a successful outcome of several years of experiments and research. The breakthrough had come when Wilbur noticed that buzzards maintain stability in the air by twisting their wing tips, and worked out that a plane could be controlled in a similar way.

Orville took this idea a step further by making the tail flexible and connecting it to the controls that altered the wings. After more painstaking experiments, a small motor and a propellor were built and fitted on to the aircraft.

The brothers received little publicity for their remarkable achievement because the newspapers did not believe that they had built and flown a plane. They spent three more years improving the design until they were able to stay up in the air for 38 minutes. After this sensational performance, the Wright brothers' plane was hailed as the greatest invention of the age and people travelled from far and wide to watch their flights.

Meanwhile other pioneers in America and Europe were also developing planes.

Otto Lilienthal

The Wright brothers were fascinated by the daring escapades of a German engineer called Otto Lilienthal. He built gliders from cotton fabric stretched across wooden ribs and jumped off cliffs, hanging underneath the aircraft. He steered by shifting the weight of his body against the wind. He crashed to his death in 1896 when the wind dropped suddenly – but his flights inspired other pioneers of the air.

Otto Lilienthal flying his glider. He made around 2,000 flights before being killed in a crash.

Orville Wright takes to the air in *Flyer*, on 17 December 1903 at Kitty Hawk, North Carolina. The fourth and final flight of the day, with Wilbur at the controls, lasted fifty-nine seconds.

Wilbur and Orville Wright

Wilbur and Orville Wright grew up in Dayton, Ohio, USA. Wilbur was born in 1867 and Orville in 1871. They became interested in flying at a very early age when their father gave them a toy helicopter. The brothers started manufacturing bicycles, but their fascination with flight persisted, and they used the workshop to make and test models to try out their ideas. After their success with the *Flyer*, the brothers went on to build and fly better planes until Wilbur died of typhoid fever in 1912. Orville gave up building aircraft after that, but when he died in 1948, he had lived long enough to see passenger airliners travelling to all parts of the world.

By 1905 the Wright brothers had developed a practical aircraft, but the American government was still not convinced by their claims. It was another three years before they were finally given a contract to build planes. They built a factory and a flying school at Dayton and went into production on a large scale. Companies were also set up in France, Germany and Britain – and so the aircraft industry was born.

In 1909 the Frenchman Louis Blériot designed a monoplane and flew across the English Channel. A month after his flight the world's first aviation meeting was held in France near Rheims. Forty different planes were displayed and Lloyd George, a British politician, commented that 'Flying machines are no longer toys and dreams; they are an established fact'.

During the First World War, planes were used to fight aerial battles. When the war ended, people began to think about peacetime flying. Two British airmen, John Alcock and Arthur Brown, achieved the first non-stop trans-Atlantic flight in 1919, at an average speed of 189.6 km an hour. Later

French aviator Louis Blériot flying over the cliffs at Dover after the first air crossing of the English Channel in 1909.

in the year the first flight from England to Australia was achieved. These flights showed the possibilities of air travel. It was not long before the first airliners were built and airline companies began operating air transport services for passengers and cargo.

In the early days of air travel, people had to dress in heavy leather coats, wear goggles and put cotton wool in their ears, to avoid being deafened by engine noise. As airline companies were established, they looked for safe, reliable aircraft to carry their passengers. The American Boeing 247D could carry ten passengers in reasonable comfort and was the forerunner of all modern airliners.

The invention of the jet engine greatly increased

the speed and altitude at which planes could fly. Planes needed to be pressurized inside because the air pressure gets lower the higher you fly. As air travel increased, and the skies became more crowded, new inventions like radar helped to improve navigation.

Almost every year passenger planes have become progressively larger, faster and more reliable, so that today they can make a thousand crossings of the Atlantic with no problems at all.

Jet engines were patented by Frank Whittle in 1930. Jet aircraft have

British aviation pioneer, Amy Johnson seated on her aircraft. She made a solo flight from England to Australia in 1930.

brought about many changes in our way of life. Tourism to all parts of the world has become a major industry. Businesses expect a quick airmail service, and many producers ship their goods by air. Perishable items (like flowers or fruit) can arrive fresh at their destination thousands of kilometres away. Aeroplanes are also a modern weapon of war.

With their invention, the Wright brothers not only fulfilled the centuries-old dream of being able to fly, they also brought all parts of the world within easy reach of one another.

The Boeing 747

The Boeing 747 is the world's largest airliner. The first 747 went into service in 1970, flying between London and New York. It had a completely new kind of engine that produced greater power, burned less fuel and made less noise. 500 people can be seated on the main deck – fifty times more than the earlier Boeing 247D. The freight version can carry 115 tonnes of cargo. The new 747-400 has an enlarged upper deck to carry more passengers. It has vertical wingtips to improve its flight performance.

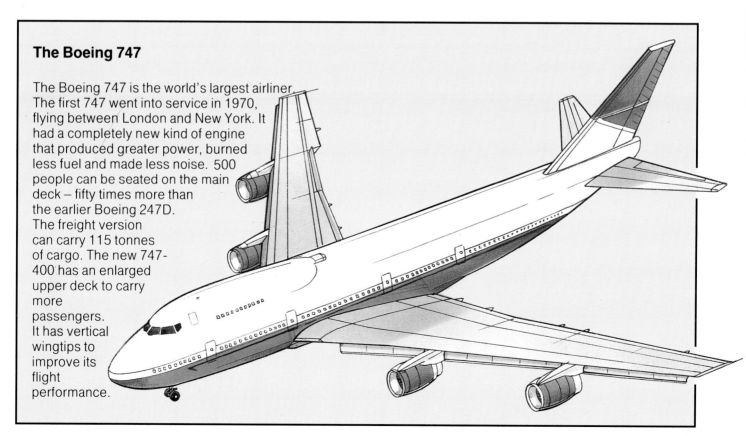

Television begins

On 2 October 1925, a revolutionary discovery was made in an attic room in London. Scotsman John Logie Baird had succeeded in transmitting a picture of a ventriloquist's dummy from one room to another. Baird ran down to the office on the ground floor and persuaded an office boy – a fifteen-year-old called Billy Taynton – to come and sit in front of his camera. Soon the boy's face appeared on a small screen, the first person in the world to be televised. That first television set was made from a biscuit tin, an old tea chest, a bicycle lamp, darning needles and some radio equipment.

Baird became famous overnight when he demonstrated his television in public. At last the money that he desperately needed was made available and he was able to improve his system. Two years later he made a transmission from London to Glasgow, and in 1928 from London to New York.

A family watching the 'Televisor', in 1930. On the screen is the head and shoulders of a man.

The British Broadcasting Corporation started the first regular television programmes using Baird's system in 1936. At the time, there were only 100 television sets to receive the pictures. Eventually a system developed in the USA, using the latest electronics, was found to give much sharper pictures and the BBC decided to adopt it instead. This was a sad blow, but nevertheless it was Baird who first made television a reality and caught the public's eye.

The Times report

On 27 January 1926, Baird demonstrated his system to members of the Royal Institution in his room in London. *The Times* newspaper reported: 'The image as transmitted was faint and often blurred but substantiated a claim that through the 'Televisor', as Mr Baird has named his apparatus, it is possible to transmit and reproduce instantly the details of movement and such things as the play of expression on the face.'

John Logie Baird adjusts his mechanical television camera. He demonstrated his television system in public for the first time in 1926, when he transmitted a small blurred picture of a ventriloquist's dummy.

John Logie Baird

John Logie Baird was born in Helensburgh, near Glasgow, Scotland in 1888. After studying science at Glasgow University he became an engineer with an electricity company, but he hated the job and wanted only to be an inventor. Several crazy inventions failed before he began to work on his apparatus for 'seeing by wireless'. When his system was rejected in favour of an electronic one, Baird turned his attention to the possibility of colour television and developed a Super Television with a giant screen. But on the day he was due to demonstrate it, in June 1946, he was taken ill with pneumonia. He died a few days later.

John Logie Baird and an early version of his television. The Nipkow disc with holes in it is on the left.

American inventor Alexander Graham Bell suggested that television might be possible some fifty years before Baird achieved the first live transmission in his attic workshop in 1925. The television system that we have today is the result of research by many inventors working in different countries. In 1880 an American, G R Carey, devised a way of using electricity to pick up the image at the back of a camera and show it a great distance away. But for even the tiniest picture, thousands of lamps and wires were needed, so his invention was not practical.

In Germany at about the same time, Paul Nipkow devised a disc that had a spiral of holes cut in it. The holes were spaced so that as the disc spun in front of a scene, a spot of light would move across the scene. By recording the light reflected from the moving spot, a picture of the scene could be reproduced. John Logie Baird was able to use a Nipkow disc in his television camera.

The next advance, the cathode-ray tube, was invented by another German, Karl Ferdinand Braun in 1897. The tube was an electronic device that produced a small spot of light on a glass screen. In 1906 a Russian scientist, Boris Rosing, realized that, by varying the brightness of the spot of light, the tube could be used to display television pictures. He used Nipkow's scanning disc to trace out the picture and convert it into an electrical signal. This signal controlled the brightness of the light spot in the cathode-ray tube. One of Rosing's students, Vladimir Zworykin, took this a step further and invented the first electronic camera tube. The all-electronic television system developed by the Marconi-EMI company in the USA used Zworykin's camera.

Television is so much a part of our daily lives that we take it for granted. Events that are happening all over the world are brought right into our living-rooms, and people in Britain and Australia can watch a live news report or sports event at the same time.

Cable networks now offer viewers a vast choice of programmes, and video recorders enable people to see their favourite shows at any time. With systems

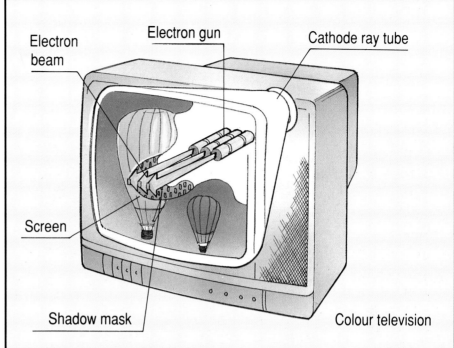

Electron beam | Electron gun | Cathode ray tube

Screen

Shadow mask | Colour television

How a television works

When a television camera films a scene, a picture forms on a small screen behind the lens. An 'electric eye' scans the screen, moving to cover every part of the picture. Each part is turned into an electric signal, and these are converted by the transmitter into radio waves. The waves are picked up by an aerial and changed back into electric signals, which pass into the television set. The television screen is the front of a cathode-ray tube. An electron gun at the back of the tube fires a beam of electricity at the screen. As the beam hits the screen, it makes tiny flashes of coloured light, which build up the picture.

like Videotext, television is increasingly being used as an information service.

In closed-circuit television, cameras are linked directly to screens and the pictures are not broadcast. These cameras are used in stores to help security staff to spot shoplifters and above roads to enable the police to monitor traffic movements.

The influence of television on our lives is enormous, and is likely to become even greater in the future. It has increased our knowledge and understanding of other cultures, and improved communication between countries. Thanks to television, we can explore the depths of the ocean (television cameras are carried in miniature submarines), or see pictures of the distant planets sent back by spacecraft. It has made the world seem like a smaller place.

The electronic age

Two days before Christmas in 1947, the first transistor was used successfully to amplify human speech. Only ten years later, more than 30 million transistors a year were being made. Now a single desk-top computer alone contains millions of transistors.

This tiny electronic device is one of the key inventions of the twentieth century. Like many of today's inventions, the transistor was the work of a team. John Bardeen and Walter Brattain, working with William Schockley at the Bell Telephone Laboratories, USA, won the Nobel Prize for physics in 1956 for this astonishing discovery.

Transistors operate as minute switches, or they can amplify an electric current. A very small current supplied to a transistor is used to control a larger one. The large current is either increased or switched off and on, by the small current. The switching takes place in less than a hundred-millionth of a second. Transistors are reliable, consume very little electricity and can be made almost unbelievably small.

Transistors are made from silicon, a cheap material that can be obtained from ordinary sand. Without transistors, the modern electronics industry would not exist.

A Mark 1 computer built in the 1950s. It took up a whole room.

Semiconductors

Walter Houser Brattain, an American physicist, worked for most of his life at the Bell Telephone Laboratories, USA. It was here that Bardeen and Brattain, under the leadership of Schockley, succeeded in making semiconductors amplify, or increase, an electric current. Semiconductors are materials that can conduct electricity. The first transistor, made from a wafer-thin slice of germanium (a semiconducting material), successfully amplified an electric current eighteen times.

The inventors of the transistor: front, William Schockley; middle, John Bardeen; right, Walter Brattain. The importance of the discovery of the transistor is that electrical currents can be amplified by this small, cheap and reliable device.

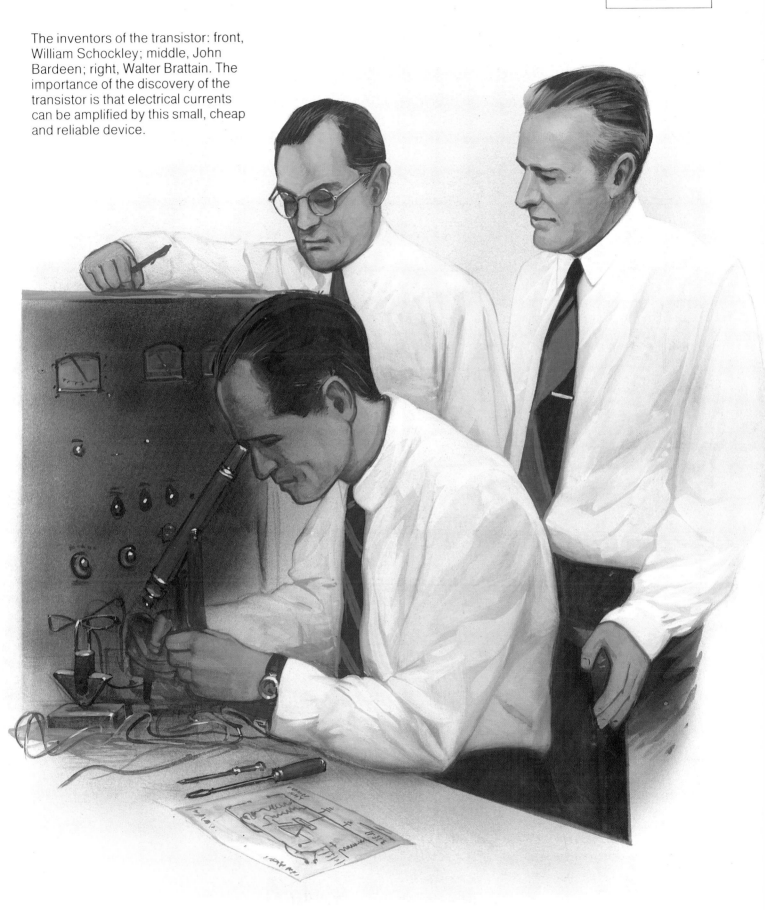

Modern electronics took off with the discovery of the transistor. Today every computer, television, pocket calculator, battery-powered watch, CD player and videocassette recorder uses transistors. All kinds of communications systems in daily use, from satellites to telephone handsets, from photo-copiers to fax machines, depend on the power of modern electronic devices.

Transistors can be made sensitive to heat or light – so they can measure temperature, or detect the presence of an intruder as part of a security system. Videocameras, night vision devices and astronomical telescopes use 'transistorized' devices to see faint stars. The

miniature laser that decodes a CD disc is a type of transistor that emits infra-red light. A similar device emits the light signals that carry telephone conversations along a fibre-optic cable.

Modern electronic devices, such as the microprocessor, developed in 1971 in the US by Ted Hoff, are based on the transistor. They are tiny, immensely complicated

A modern aircraft relies on electronic control systems. Some planes could fly without pilots.

The invention of microprocessors has made possible very complex, compact machines such as this robot hand.

and very costly to develop. But they can be manufactured by the million and are therefore sold cheaply. If they are faulty, they can easily be replaced. They depend on very simple principles – a transistor provides a way of using a small electric current to control a larger one. Group the transistors together, and there is no limit to what can be done. You can even use them to pilot a spaceship.

Two Nobel prizes

John Bardeen, an American physicist, is remarkable because he received two Nobel Prizes for physics. The first he shared with Brattain and Schockley in 1956 for their joint development of the transistor. The second prize in 1972, which he also shared, was for the development of the first theory that explained superconductivity. This is the ability of metals and some other materials to lose all electrical resistance at very low temperatures. Now scientists all over the world are researching superconductivity.

A second Industrial Revolution

The Industrial Revolution is the name given to the time when machines replaced muscle power in industries. The new steam engine could do the work of horses or many people. The changes that occurred accelerated our knowledge of the material world, and modern science began. The Electronic Age has been called the Second Industrial Revolution – there are now machines that increase thinking and calculating power enormously. This new age may increase our understanding of the human mind.

Glossary

Acid rain Rain that becomes more acid when it mixes with waste gases in the atmosphere.

Alloy A mixture of two or more metals. Brass is an alloy of copper and zinc.

Biplane An aeroplane with two sets of wings, one above the other.

Carbon dioxide A gas which we breathe out and that is given out by power stations. Too much carbon dioxide in the atmosphere is thought to cause global warming.

Cathode-ray tube The part of a television set that produces the picture.

Chip A small electronic circuit made on a piece of semiconductor material, such as silicon. Also called a silicon chip.

Compact disc (CD) A disc on which sound is recorded and replayed by laser.

Condenser The part of a steam engine that turns steam back into water.

Cylinder A hollow tube with vertical sides. Engines burn their fuel inside cylinders.

Database A computerized system for storing and retrieving information.

Dynamo A device for converting mechanical energy into electricity. Dynamos, also called generators, are used in electricity power stations.

Filament The long, thin coiled wire in an electric light bulb.

Fossil fuels Sources of energy like coal, oil and gas, formed from the remains of life that existed many millions of years ago.

Germanium A crystalline substance used to make the first transistors.

Infra-red rays Invisible heat rays given out by every hot object.

Laser A device that produces an intense beam of light of one colour.

Microprocessor A series of microelectronic circuits all etched into one single, tiny chip of silicon.

Molecule A group of atoms linked together. Atoms are tiny particles that form the structure of matter.

Monoplane The more modern design of aeroplane, having one set of wings.

Patent The sole right to make, use and sell an invention.

Radar A type of radio that gives an image of a distant object on a screen.

Radio valve A device used to control an electric current or switch it on and off. Valves were used in early radios before transistors were invented.

Semiconductors A material that conducts electricity, but not as efficiently as a metal. Semiconductors are used to make transistors and electronic chips.

Static A crackling sound heard on a radio during an electrical storm, or caused by electrical equipment.

Stereophonic sound Realistic sound produced from two loudspeakers.

Superconductor A metal or alloy which conducts electricity without resistance.

Telex An electrically operated typewriter used for sending or receiving messages.

Transformer A device that increases or decreases the electrical voltage of an electric current.

Transmitter A device that sends out radio signals which can be received by another radio.

Type Pieces of metal with raised, reversed images of letters on them, once widely used for printing.

Vacuum An empty space in which there is no air.

Videotext Information transmitted by a television station that can be displayed on an adapted television screen.

Further reading

Conquest of the Air, David Jefferis (Franklin Watts, 1990)

George Stephenson and the Industrial Revolution, Jason Hook (Wayland, 1987)

Invention (Eyewitness Guides), Lionel Bender (Dorling Kindersley, 1991)

The Inventions that Changed the World, Gordon Rattray Taylor (Readers Digest, 1982)

Mothers of Invention, Ethlie Ann Vare and Greg Ptacek, (Quill, 1987) (A book for older pupils and adults. It looks at the contribution women have made to the history of inventions.)

The Triumph of Invention, Trevor I Williams (Macdonald Orbis, 1987)

Twenty Inventors, Jacqueline Dineen (Wayland, 1988)

The Wright Brothers, Jason Hook (Wayland, 1989)

See also Wayland's *Pioneers of Science* series, which includes titles on Bell, Benz, Edison, Faraday, Marconi and Watt.

Timeline

Major inventions, including those discussed in this book.

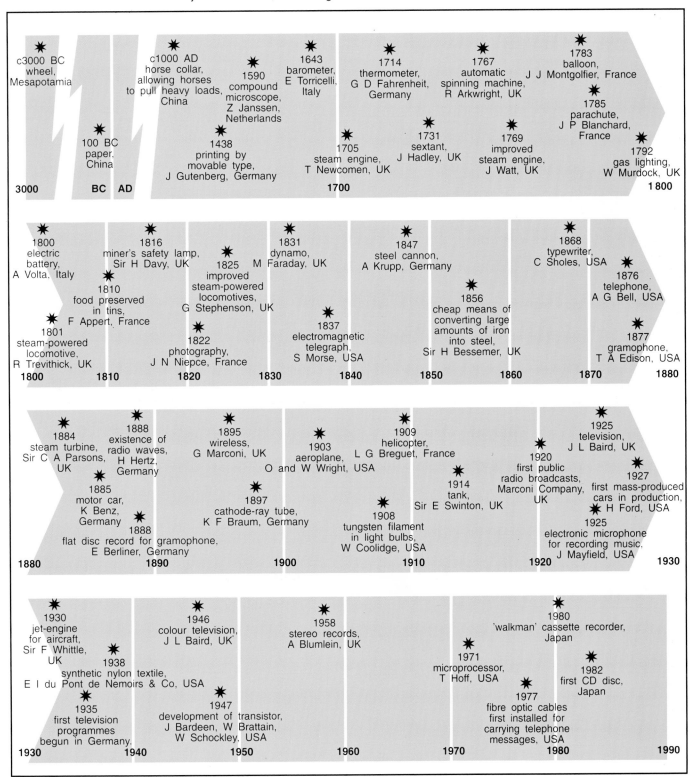

c3000 BC
wheel,
Mesapotamia

100 BC
paper,
China

c1000 AD
horse collar,
allowing horses
to pull heavy loads
China

1438
printing by
movable type,
J Gutenberg, Germany

1590
compound
microscope,
Z Janssen,
Netherlands

1643
barometer,
E Torricelli,
Italy

1705
steam engine,
T Newcomen, UK

1714
thermometer,
G D Fahrenheit,
Germany

1731
sextant,
J Hadley, UK

1767
automatic
spinning machine,
R Arkwright, UK

1769
improved
steam engine,
J Watt, UK

1783
balloon,
J J Montgolfier, France

1785
parachute,
J P Blanchard,
France

1792
gas lighting,
W Murdock, UK

3000   **BC** **AD**   **1700**   **1800**

1800
electric
battery,
A Volta, Italy

1801
steam-powered
locomotive,
R Trevithick, UK

1810
food preserved
in tins,
F Appert, France

1816
miner's safety lamp,
Sir H Davy, UK

1822
photography,
J N Niepce, France

1825
improved
steam-powered
locomotives,
G Stephenson, UK

1831
dynamo,
M Faraday, UK

1837
electromagnetic
telegraph,
S Morse, USA

1847
steel cannon,
A Krupp, Germany

1856
cheap means of
converting large
amounts of iron
into steel,
Sir H Bessemer, UK

1868
typewriter,
C Sholes, USA

1876
telephone,
A G Bell, USA

1877
gramophone,
T A Edison, USA

1800   **1810**   **1820**   **1830**   **1840**   **1850**   **1860**   **1870**   **1880**

1884
steam turbine,
Sir C A Parsons,
UK

1885
motor car,
K Benz,
Germany

1888
flat disc record for gramophone,
E Berliner, Germany

1888
existence of
radio waves,
H Hertz,
Germany

1895
wireless,
G Marconi, UK

1897
cathode-ray tube,
K F Braum, Germany

1903
aeroplane,
O and W Wright, USA

1908
tungsten filament
in light bulbs,
W Coolidge, USA

1909
helicopter,
L G Breguet, France

1914
tank,
Sir E Swinton, UK

1920
first public
radio broadcasts,
Marconi Company,
UK

1925
television,
J L Baird, UK

1925
electronic microphone
for recording music,
J Mayfield, USA

1927
first mass-produced
cars in production,
H Ford, USA

1880   **1890**   **1900**   **1910**   **1920**   **1930**

1930
jet-engine
for aircraft,
Sir F Whittle,
UK

1935
first television
programmes
begun in Germany.

1938
synthetic nylon textile,
E I du Pont de Nemoirs & Co, USA

1946
colour television,
J L Baird, UK

1947
development of transistor,
J Bardeen, W Brattain,
W Schockley, USA

1958
stereo records,
A Blumlein, UK

1971
microprocessor,
T Hoff, USA

1977
fibre optic cables
first installed for
carrying telephone
messages, USA

1980
'walkman' cassette recorder,
Japan

1982
first CD disc,
Japan

1930   **1940**   **1950**   **1960**   **1970**   **1980**   **1990**

Index